FEAR NOT!

I0170435

BY

SKIP BLYTHE

Fear Not!

Copyright © 2013 by John I. Blythe

Published by:

Oak of Acadiana Publications
18896 Greenwell Springs Road
Greenwell Springs, Louisiana 70739
www.ThePublishedWord.com

Oak of Acadiana Publications is a publishing imprint of McDougal & Associates, an organization dedicated to the spreading the Gospel of the Lord Jesus Christ to as many people as possible in the shortest time possible.

ISBN 978-1-940461-00-7

Printed on demand in the U.S., the UK, and Australia
For worldwide distribution

FEAR NOT!

Oak of Acadiana Publications
18896 Greenwell Springs Road
Greenwell Springs, LA 70739
www.thepublishedword.com

For God has not given us a spirit of fear, but of power and of love and of a sound mind. 2 Timothy 1:7

Fear not, little flock; for it is your Father's good pleasure to give you the kingdom. Luke 12:32

CONTENTS

INTRODUCTION

FEAR … It is the biggest hindrance to your peace.

FEAR … It is the biggest hindrance to your joy.

FEAR … It is the biggest hindrance to your success in life.

But there is good news.

Fear can be controlled.

Fear can be reduced.

Fear can be destroyed.

Is there a secret to eliminating fear?

Oh, yes, there is! But, truth be told, it's not really a secret. It has been under your nose all the time. It may have been sitting on your coffee table. It may have been sitting on your bookshelf. You may have used it every single day and not realized that it contained the secret to a life free from fear.

Can you imagine such a life? Wouldn't it be wonderful? Each of us would benefit from it.

Well, what can provide you with freedom from fear? The answer is simply the Bible. Yes, the Bible, the Word of God!

You may say, "Oh, come on, I've heard that before. That's easier said than done." Or you may say, "Oh, tell me something new." But there is no other answer to fear.

Why can I say that the Bible has the answer to controlling fear? Because God used men who were inspired by the Holy Spirit to write every single page of it. They wrote what the Holy Spirit told them to write, and only God has the answer for fear. So let us ask God what to do about the fear in our lives that robs us of His very best, and let us see what He answers us.

Skip Blythe
Greenwell Springs, Louisiana

Chapter 1

God's Declaration Concerning Fear

God hath not given us the spirit of fear; but of power, and of love, and of a sound mind. 2 Timothy 1:7

There can be no doubt about God's attitude toward fear. He emphatically states in His Word that He did not give us the spirit of fear, and He does not want us to be fearful.

This word *fear,* in the original Greek, means "timidity, fearfulness, cowardice." God did not give us such things.

What did He give us? He gave us power, love, and a sound mind. This word *power* in the Hebrew means "strength, power, ability." Included in this definition are "* inherent power, power residing in a thing by virtue of its nature, or which a person or thing exerts and puts forth. * power for performing miracles; * moral power and excellence of soul; * the power and influence which belongs to riches and wealth; * power and resources arising from numbers; * power consisting in or resting upon armies, forces, hosts." God wants us to have the power to overcome fear.

The word *love* in this context simply means "affection, good will, benevolence, brotherly love."

A *sound mind* means "an admonishing or calling to soundness of mind, to moderation and self-control." I emphasize these points because these represent the spirit God does give us. And these things will conquer fear and cause us to be triumphant and successful in life.

God's Word promises:

There is no fear in love; but perfect love casteth out fear: because fear hath tor- ment. He that feareth is not made perfect in love. 1 John 4:18

Casteth (or casts) means "to throw or let go of a thing without caring where it falls." Perfect love will allow you to let go of your fears, to throw them away without caring where they fall.

What is *perfect love*? The answer may be in the second part of the verse, which says: *"He that feareth is not made perfect in love."* So, how are we made perfect in love?

What does the Bible say about love? It says a lot on this all-important subject. Let's look at one scripture in particular in John's first letter to the churches. To get the whole picture and context, we must begin reading at verse 7:

13

7 Beloved, let us love one another: for love is of God; and everyone that loveth is born of God, and knoweth God. He that loveth not knoweth not God; for God is love. In this was manifested the love of God toward us, because that God sent His only begotten Son into the world, that we might live through Him. Herein is love, not that we loved God, but that He loved us, and sent His Son to be the propitiation for our sins. 11 Beloved, if God so loved us, we ought also to love one another. 12 No man hath seen God at any time. If we love one another, God dwelleth in us, and His love is perfected in us. 13 Hereby know that we dwell in Him, and He is us, because He hath given us His Spirit. 14 And we have seen and do testify that the Father sent the Son to be the Savior of the world. 15 Whosoever shall confess that Jesus is the Son of God, God dwelleth in him, and he in God. 16 And we have known and believed the love that God hath to us. God is love; and he that dwelleth in love dwelleth in God, and God in him. 17 Herein is our love made perfect, that we may have boldness in the day of judgment: because as He is, so are we in this world.

1 John 4:7-17

Again, in verse 18, it says *"Perfect love casts out fear; and, he that fears is not made perfect in love."*

Who among us has never felt fear? We must conclude that every person born into this world has experienced it at one time or another. But God has a remedy.

There is a revelation of truth in these scriptures. We can read the words over and over, as many of us have our whole lives, and still miss the importance of what was written for our benefit.

To encapsulate these verses, we are encouraged to love one another because

15

God is love, and those who love are born from Him and know Him. If we don't love others, then we don't really know God, because God is love. God's love for us was demonstrated by the Father sending His only begotten Son to the earth to pay the penalty for our sin, so that we could live our lives through Him.

It makes sense that if God loved us so much that He gave His Son, Jesus, to die for our sins, then we should love one another. If we love one another, then we know that God's Spirit lives within us, and His love is perfected in us. This is that *"perfect love"* which *"casts out all fear."*

Let's go a little further, because there is a deep truth in these scriptures. We know that we live in God, and He lives in us because He has given us His Spirit, and we believe that the Father sent His Son, Jesus, to be the Savior of the world. If we confess that Jesus is the Son of God, then we know that He lives in us, and we live in Him. We know that God is love, and if we live in love for others, then we live in God, and God lives in us.

Verse 17 tells us that because we know that God is love, we are in Him and He is in us, so that our love is made *"perfect,"* and we can have boldness in the Day of Judgment. Perfect love casts out all fear, including the fear of judgment.

How many of us have lived with a sense of impending doom? How many of us have felt that God would harshly judge us one day because of our sin? Fear not, my brother and sister, for God is love. God loves you, and His Spirit in you has given you the ability to be bold and not live under the constant fear of judgment.

In my opinion, although verse 18 primarily has to do with the fear or judgment, it also relates to all fear. Remember that perfect love casts out fear and that you have the ability to love those whom you may consider unlovely or undeserving of love. To consider any person to be undeserving of love is not a Christian attitude at all, but it happens — unfortunately.

If you are a born-again Christian, you have the ability to love even those who have done you harm. Jesus said:

But I say unto you, love your enemies, bless them that curse you, do good to them that hate you, and pray for them which despite-fully use you, and persecute you.
                                    Matthew 5:44

As a child of God, you have the ability to walk in a lifestyle of *"perfect love,"* and therefore, you have the ability to live a life FREE FROM FEAR!

Chapter 2

Fear Is Common To All

Fear not, little flock; for it is your Father's good pleasure to give you the kingdom.

Luke 12:32

Fear is common to all. God knows this well and has been saying to His people throughout the ages, *"Fear not."*

God told Abram, whose name was changed to Abraham, *"Fear not"*:

Fear not , Abram: I am thy shield, and thy exceeding great reward.   Genesis 15:1

God told Isaac, Abraham's son, *"Fear not"*:

Fear not, for I am with thee, and will bless thee, and multiply thy seed for my servant Abraham's sake.   Genesis 26:24

God told Jacob, whose name was changed to Israel, *"Fear not"*:

I am God, the God of thy father: fear not to go down into Egypt; for I will there make of thee a great nation.   Genesis 46:3

God told Joshua, who was to lead the people of Israel into their Promised Land, *"Fear not!"*:

Fear not or be dismayed…. . Be strong and of good courage.   Joshua 8:1

God told Ruth, King David's grand-mother, *"Fear not"*:

And now, my daughter, fear not; I will do to thee all that thou requirest.

Ruth 3:11

God told the prophet Daniel, *"Fear not":*

Then said he unto me, Fear not, Daniel.

Daniel 10:12

These are all Old Testament characters, but the same thing continued to happen in New Testament times. Throughout the Bible, God told His people not to fear because He was with them and for them. He "had their back," as we commonly say today.

When Jesus eventually came, His message was the same:

And he laid his right hand upon me [John], saying unto me, Fear not; I am the first and the last. Revelation 1:17

Thank God, He is still telling you and me today, "Fear not," because He is greater than any enemy (real or imagined) that could possibly come against us. We are not to fear because our God desires to give us the very best.

Hear His voice today, saying to you:

Fear not, little flock; for it is your Father's good pleasure to give you the kingdom.

Luke 12:32

Chapter 3

My Own Struggle with Fear

Fear hath torment. 1 John 4:18

Years ago, when I and my family were serving as missionaries in the Juarez, Mexico area, we made the trip back and forth to Baton Rouge (our home) many times a year over Interstate 10. Less than an hour outside of the capital city, there is a very high bridge over what is known as Whiskey Bay. On one of those trips, after I had been driving for about seventeen hours straight, when I got to the top of that bridge, I was suddenly paralyzed with fear — for no apparent reason.

In my mind, I felt that I could somehow be controlled by an unknown force and caused to swerve and go off of that bridge. I know it doesn't make sense, and I can't explain it, but my whole body suddenly tensed, and all my muscles tightened. As crazy as it sounds, it was a very real fear.

I could not wait to get to the other side of that bridge, and I was praying the whole time for God to deliver us, and asking Him to rebuke Satan. I was terrified.

I didn't tell my wife and young daughter about this incidence until much later, for I was embarrassed that I could give in to an irrational fear to such a degree. And it didn't end there. From that time on, for a while, I dreaded going over that bridge. I am happy to say that I eventually got victory over that fear, through praying and quoting the promises of the Word of God.

One scripture that I quoted was the one we talked about already:

*God has not given us the spirit of fear, but
of power and love and a sound mind.*
2 Timothy 1:7

Also, I would repeat the first part of
Isaiah 54:17:

*No weapon that is formed against thee
shall prosper ... .*

The enemy had formed the weapon of
fear in my mind, and I had imagined a
tragedy that could not have happened un-
less I had given in to that irrational fear. By
entertaining that foolish fear, I was giving
the enemy power that he did not actually
possess.

Fear is real, whether the thing we fear
is imagined or real. In fact, the Bible says,
"fear hath torment" (1 John 4:18), and I
can readily agree with that assessment!
This word *torment* in the Greek means

"correction, punishment, and penalty." No one wants these things.

As I noted at the outset, fear is the biggest hindrance to our peace, our joy, and our success. Fear is an obstacle to us enjoying the wonderful world God has provided for us. Fear keeps some people in their homes, because of an imagined terror that *might* happen to them if they dare to go out. Fear keeps some from flying in airplanes, or riding in buses, trains, cars, or boats. Fear is behind phobias too numerous to mention.

Phobias are caused by an imagined fear of danger or doom. *Webster's Dictionary* defines *phobia* as "an exaggerated, usually inexplicable and illogical fear of a particular object, class of objects, or situation." But as exaggerated, inexplicable, and illogical as such fears might be, they are still common.

Why is that? Fear is the opposite of faith. Having faith in God proves that we trust Him, and fear proves that we don't. So discovering how to overcome fear is very important to each of us.

Let's look first at this word *trust*. The Bible says:

Trust in the Lord with all thine heart, and lean not unto thine own understanding. In all thy ways acknowledge Him, and He shall direct thy paths.   Proverbs 3:5-6

As a child, did you ever jump into your father's arms at a pool? Did you hesitate? You probably just jumped, right? You trusted your dad to catch you? How much more should we trust our heavenly Father to catch us in times of need?

God's Word promises:

The God of my rock; in him will I trust: he is my shield, and the horn of my salvation,

*my high tower and my refuge, my savior;
thou savest me from violence.*

2 Samuel 22:3

*Some trust in chariots, and some in hors-
es: but we will remember the name of the
Lord our God.* Psalm 20:7

These days we might say, "Some trust
in money, and some in government; some
trust in business and some in armies, but
we, as Christians, will remember the name
of the Lord our God."

The psalmist declared:

*Oh my God, I trust in thee: let me not be
ashamed, let not mine enemies triumph
over me.* Psalm 37:5

*Commit thy way unto the Lord; trust also
in him; and he shall bring it to pass.*

Psalm 25:2

Throughout the Bible, we are admonished to trust in God and promised that with that trust will come blessing.

The word *trust* in the original Hebrew has many meanings, depending on the context of the verse in which it is used. Sometimes it means "to have confidence in, to be bold, to be secure, or to feel safe." In other cases it means "to seek refuge or flee for protection; to confide or hope in God." When we feel hopeless, when we feel sad or grieved, when we feel afraid, when we feel overwhelmed, when we feel out of control, we need to remember the promises of our God contained in the Holy Scriptures:

Humble yourselves therefore under the mighty hand of God, that he may exalt you in due time: casting all of your care upon him; for he careth for you. 1 Peter 5:6-7

This word *careth*, as used in this verse, in the Greek means simply "to care about." What is the significance of this meaning? In other words, when we humble ourselves and cast our cares (our concerns) on God, then He cares for us. He does the "caring" for us. It doesn't just mean that He takes care of us; it also means that He takes care of our concerns for us – if we trust Him to do so.

God is so good! We have to wonder how He could love us as He does. The answer is that He not only *has* love, but He *is* love, and so He will do the caring for you.

Many times I have had to examine myself to see if I was truly trusting the Lord. I said that I trusted Him, and I sang that I trusted Him, but at times my actions said something very different. When everything was going well, when times were good, I felt that I trusted Him. But, just let things turn bad and suddenly things were not going so right at the moment, and I couldn't help but notice what happened. I am embarrassed to admit that I have sometimes found myself lacking in trust at such moments.

What was happening? One moment I said that I trusted God, but within seconds, my actions proved otherwise. This shows what a constant battle it is for all of us to be strong in faith and resist all fear. It requires a daily struggle with our natural thinking, a struggle to believe and rely upon the promises of God.

How many of you can relate to this problem? Personally, as I've already stated, I think it is common to all mankind. And how do we overcome this back and forth of our thinking?

I have tried in my own ability and with prayer to live in constant trust, no matter what the circumstances, and have often come up short. If this has been your experience too, then we must all look to the Scriptures for an answer.

I encourage you to study the Word of God as you are reading this book, for the Scriptures teach us:

Study to show thyself approved unto God, a workman that needeth not to be ashamed, rightly dividing the word of truth.   2 Timothy 2:15

What do we have to lose? If God has the answer for fear, then we want it.

CHAPTER 4

FAITH IS THE PRIME FACTOR IN OVERCOMING FEAR

Without faith, it is impossible to please Him because he that comes to God must first believe that He is and also that He is a re-warder of those who diligently seek Him. Hebrews 11:6

To my way of thinking, faith in God is the prime factor that needs our attention here, so we must build our trust in Him. The Bible tells us that without faith we cannot please Him.

In order to please God, we must first believe that He exists and also that He rewards those who diligently seek Him. *Rewarder*, in the Greek, means "one who pays wages."

The word *diligently* is self-explanatory. It means for us to seek God with all our heart, mind, will, and emotions. It means that we should strive to get to know Him and His ways better. We do this through prayer, praise, and worship, meditation, and the study of His Word – the Holy Bible.

Going to church is also important, but it is not enough to enable us to grow as a Christian and to gain faith, and gaining in our faith is the only thing that will produce trust in God and victory over fear.

So, how do we increase our faith in order to build our trust in God? The Bible says:

So then faith cometh by hearing, and hearing by the word of God.

Romans 10:17

The word *hearing* here simply means "to hear with our ears." It's that simple. Faith comes by hearing the Word of God, by hearing the Gospel or Good News found in the Word of God, the Bible.

The Gospel (Good News) is simply that we don't have to die spiritually for our sins because Jesus Christ died for us. He died in our place so that we could live forever with the Father, Jesus, and the Holy Spirit in Heaven.

The plan of salvation is found throughout the Bible and culminates with the death, burial, and resurrection of Christ. He is our Savior.

The Word of God found in the Bible is Good News to those who will believe it. It gives hope to the hopeless. It gives joy to those who mourn. It gives peace to those who are tormented. When we hear the Word of God through preaching, when we read and study the Word of God in our personal time, when we meditate on the Word of God and His goodness to us, then our faith increases. When our faith increases, then our trust level increases. And when we trust God, our fears diminish.

Like many of you, I love the 23rd Psalm:

Yea, though I walk through the valley of the shadow of death, I will fear no evil: for thou art with me; thy rod and thy staff they comfort me. Thou preparest a table before me in the presence of mine enemies: thou anointest my head with oil; my cup runneth over. Surely goodness and mercy shall follow me all the days of my life: and I will dwell in the house of the LORD forever. Psalm 23:4-6

This word *valley*, in the original Hebrew, means "a steep, narrow gorge." The idea is like sheep going through a dangerous narrow gorge where predators can easily attack them.

The sheep are led by a shepherd, Who is none other than the Lord God Himself. Even though this is a place of fear and the shadow of death, the sheep trust in the Shepherd because they are protected by His rod and His staff. Therefore, even though the valley is a place of extreme distress and danger, the sheep fear no evil.

The shadow of death is a place of darkness and fear, and yet Jesus said:

The people which sat in darkness saw great light; and to them which sat in the region and shadow of death light is sprung up.   Matthew 4:16

When John the Baptist came into the world, he was spoken of as *"the prophet of the Highest,"* even though he was just a child:

> *And thou, child, shalt be called the prophet of the Highest: for thou shalt go before the face of the Lord to prepare his ways; to give knowledge of salvation unto his people by the remission of their sins, through the tender mercy of our God; whereby the dayspring from on high hath visited us, to give light to them that sit in darkness and in the shadow of death, to guide our feet into the way of peace.*
>
> Luke 1:76-79

In *"the shadow of death,"* we are to fear *"no evil"* because our Great Shepherd is with us. He is there constantly to protect us from all enemies.

As believers, our enemies are not flesh and blood; they are spiritual enemies who desire to destroy our souls. God has given us spiritual armor and a weapon to use against our adversary, the devil. We use this armor and weapon in prayer by the power invested in us by the Holy Spirit of God. Let us learn more about our spiritual armor and our spiritual weapons.

CHAPTER 5

DONNING OUR SPIRITUAL ARMOR

Finally, my brethren, be strong in the Lord, and in the power of His might. Put on the whole Armour of God, that ye may be able to stand against the wiles of the devil. For we wrestle not against flesh and blood, but against principalities, against powers, against the rulers of the darkness of this world, against spiritual wickedness in high (places). Wherefore take unto you the whole Armour of God, that ye may be able to withstand in the evil day, and having done all, to stand. Stand therefore, having your loins girt about with truth,

*and having on the breastplate of righteous-
ness; and your feet shod with the preparation of the gospel of peace; above all, taking
the shield of faith, wherewith ye shall be
able to quench all the fiery darts of the
wicked. And take the helmet of salvation,
and the sword of the Spirit, which is the
Word of God.*   Ephesians 6:10-17

Paul explained the armor God has provided for us in his letter to the Ephesians.
It is worth the effort to study these verses.
If we look at them more closely, we can get
a clearer understanding of what the writer
is saying:

First of all, we are admonished to *"be
strong in the Lord and in the power of his
might."* God is our strength and our power.
He makes our way perfect. He makes our
feet like those of a mountain deer, and He
sets us on our high places. We are never
encouraged to live in our own strength,

because it always fails. God wants us to be strong *"in Him"* and in the power of *"His might."*

THE GIRDLE OF TRUTH

There are many scriptures in the Bible in which God tells His people to be strong in Him. Then, after He tells us to be strong, He tells us how to do it. He says that we must put on the whole armor of God, covering ourselves, beginning with our loins.

Paul was not talking here about our physical loins. The loins represent the procreative part of the body. What he is saying is that we must have our loins girded with truth. This clearly has to do with our minds, because that is where we understand truth. Through these words God is saying that we need to gird up our minds with the belt of truth, to fasten truth around the mental, or procreative part of our body, which is the mind.

Peter wrote something very similar in his first letter to the churches:

Gird up the loins of your mind.

1 Peter 1:13

Remember the first scripture mentioned at the beginning of the book, that God has not given us the spirit of fear, but of power, love, and a sound mind. God wants our minds to be strengthened with truth. The mind is what controls everything that we do, so it is very important that we guard our minds.

Mark wrote that we are to love the Lord our God with our whole mind:

And thou shalt love the Lord thy God with all thy heart, and with all thy soul,

and with all thy mind, and with all thy strength: this is the first commandment.
                                                    Mark 12:30

In Romans, Paul stated that the *"carnal [fleshly, human nature] mind is enmity [hatred] against God"* (Romans 8:7). In that book, he also admonished us not to be conformed to this world, but to be transformed *"by the renewing of [our] mind[s]"* (Romans 12:1).

In Ephesians, Paul tells us to be renewed in the strength of our minds (Ephesians 4:23). In 2 Corinthians, he teaches us to be in unity as Christians, or to be *"of one mind"* (2 Corinthians 13:11). So you can see how important it is, in our battle against spiritual enemies, to strengthen the procreative part of our body – the mind. And the way we put on the armor for the mind is by reading and studying God's Word.

45

THE BREASTPLATE OF RIGHTEOUSNESS

Another piece of the armor that God tells us to put on in order to effectively defeat the author of fear is *"the breastplate of righteousness"* (Ephesians 6:14). Although this verse calls it a *"breastplate of righteousness,"* 1 Thessalonians 5:8 calls it a *"breastplate of faith."*

The typical ancient breastplate consisted of two parts, and it protected the body on both sides from the neck to the mid section.

The word *righteousness* in this application simply means "a condition acceptable to God; integrity, virtue, purity of life, rightness, correctness of thinking, feeling and acting." In 1 Thessalonians, where it is called a *"breastplate of faith,"* the word *faith* means "conviction of truth and belief respecting man's relationship to God and divine things; generally with the included idea of trust and holy fervor born of faith and joined with it."

One of the vital organs a breastplate protected was the heart. Without the physical heart pumping blood, we couldn't survive. In a spiritual sense, the heart has to do with faithfulness, fidelity, belief, trust, and faith. We are told in the Scriptures to comfort, prepare, establish, and purify our hearts and never to harden them.

The mind and the heart are connected in scripture, and Proverbs declares:

As he [a man] thinketh in his heart, so he is.   Proverbs 23:7

We also put this part of the armor on by reading and studying the Word of God.

THE SHOES OF PEACE

Another protection provided by the armor of God is for the feet. It may seem strange to protect your feet in order to do battle against spiritual enemies, but Ephesians 6:15 clearly says that we must have our *"feet shod with the preparation of the gospel of peace."* The word *foot* in this application, in the original Greek, had to do with putting the foot on the vanquished. It also relates to disciples listening to their teacher's instruction at his feet.

The word *shod* means "to under-bind; to bind under one's self." Isaiah said:

How beautiful on the mountains are the feet of him that bringeth good tidings, that publisheth peace; that bringeth good tidings of good, that publisheth salvation; that saith unto Zion, Thy God reigneth.
Isaiah 52:7

The prophet Nahum said:

Behold upon the mountains the feet of him that bringeth good tidings, that publisheth peace! Nahum 1:15

The feet are very important to us, as humans, because they provide us with mobility and get us where we are going. They are also important to God in a spiritual sense. The word *feet* occurs 256 times in the King James Bible, so this shows how important to God the feet are.

Moses was told by God to take his shoes off of his feet because the place he stood on was holy ground. God later told Moses that everywhere the soles of his feet would tread would be his.

God told Joshua that when the soles of the feet of the priests bearing the arc touched the waters of the Jordan river, those waters would part. God later told Joshua to put his feet on the necks of some defeated enemy kings and that wherever his feet would tread would belong to him and his children forever.

In the New Testament, Jesus told His disciples that when they went out preaching the Gospel of peace and they were rejected, to shake the dust off of their feet as a testimony against their detractors. This can be found in Matthew 10:14, Mark 6:11, Luke 9:5, and Acts 13:51.

God sends His love to the lost by sending His servants to bring them the Good News of salvation.

Romans 1:16 say:

For I am not ashamed of the gospel of Christ: for it is the power of God unto salvation to every one that believeth; to the Jew first, and also to the Greek.

There is *"power,"* or strength, in truth. Therefore, it is important to cover the feet with the proper spiritual armor.

When the people we witness to choose to reject God's love, we are told to shake off the dust from our feet against them. And one day God will cause Satan himself to be bruised under our feet:

And the God of peace shall bruise Satan under your feet shortly. Romans 16:20

So, we can see how important it is to God that our armor, as Christians, include something to protect our feet. This is another level of protection from the enemy in order to give us boldness and freedom from fear.

THE SHIELD OF FAITH

Another protection included in the armor of God is the shield of faith. This is also mentioned in Ephesians 6:16. That verse says, *"Above all, taking the shield of faith."*

This shield of faith is a protection against the fiery darts of the wicked. The wicked, who are our spiritual enemies and are led by Satan, are "hell bent" on destroying us.

Satan's desire is to cause Christians to give up hope. He wants us destroyed. He wants us inept, unable to declare the truths of the Gospel. He wants to keep us bound in fear and apathy. He does not want us to be bold in our proclamation of what God has done in us and for us.

Satan is also happy to see Christians turn on themselves. He is happy to see "religious" and judgmental Christians, who are just going through the motions and not making a positive impact on the world around them. Satan does not mind Christians who go to church every Sunday, only to leave the church and go back to their carnal ways. It doesn't bother him to see Christians sing their songs and make lofty prayers in church, if they will then leave the church building and start gossiping about other believers.

Satan loves a crippled church. He is called a thief in John 10:10, where his goal is revealed. He has come to *"steal, kill and destroy,"* and he is good at it.

The shield of faith is a protection against the fiery darts of the wicked. Fiery darts are like spiritual burning arrows shot from the bows of demonic enemies toward us. Faith, which is the opposite of fear, will protect us against these arrows, as the psalmist declared:

> *I will not be afraid for the terror by night; nor for the arrow that flieth by day; nor for the pestilence that walketh in darkness; nor for the destruction that wasteth at noonday. A thousand shall fall at thy side, and ten thousand at thy right hand; but it shall not come nigh thee.*
>
> Psalm 91:5-7

The reason we are protected is that we are under God's feathers and wings, as mentioned in verse 4. I love the first verse of this psalm:

He that dwelleth in the secret place of the most High shall abide under the shadow of the almighty.　　　　Psalm 91:1

David said, in Psalm 57:1, that his soul trusted in God and that he would make his refuge in the shadow of His wings. It takes faith, which is a shield, to keep us under the shadow of the Almighty!

But isn't that an awesome promise? He who remains in the secret place of the most High will live under the shadow of the Almighty. You could write a whole book on just this verse alone.

Satan's fiery darts are sent to destroy us. They are sent to cause fear in us. They are aimed at our minds, bodies, and spirits.

If we accept his lies, fear paralyzes us. It causes doubt in our minds. That is why we need the shield of faith.

Faith says that no weapon formed against us will prosper. Faith declares that I can do all things through Christ who strengthens me. When we raise up the shield of faith through our proclamation and actions, it causes our enemies to be confused and to either stop their attacks or to pause to regroup. When we come under spiritual attack and are victorious through our faith, we must always keep our shields up.

The enemy is like a roaring lion, seeking whom he may devour. So the more our faith can grow, the stronger and more successful we will become.

Faith is one of the most important protections and weapons against the attacks of the enemy. As we noted, the Bible says that without faith it is impossible to please God because we must first believe that God *is* and that He is a rewarder of those who diligently seek Him.

Our whole Christian life is based on our level of faith. Faith sees the answer in the Spirit realm before it is manifested in the natural.

We are told, in the Scriptures, to speak to the things that are not as though they were (see Roman 4:17). Jesus said, *"Only believe,"* (Mark 5:36). Our belief in God and Jesus, the Messiah, is based on what the Father did by providing His Son as a sacrifice for our sins, but it requires that we believe that is what He did:

> *Believe on the Lord Jesus Christ and thou shalt be saved.*   Acts 16:31

Faith is belief. With faith you can say to the mountains in your life to be removed and cast into the sea, and they will obey you. Jesus told many people who were sick that their faith had made them whole. We are to believe, without doubting, that God will answer our prayers, and He will. Doubt says that we don't believe that He will, so He won't.

How soon do you expect answers to your prayers? Immediately? Sometimes the answers come instantly, and sometimes they don't. God wants us to be patient and trust Him in all situations.

God wants our faith to be unwavering:

Let us hold fast the profession of our faith without wavering; (for he is faithful that promised).   Hebrews 10:23

God has made many promises to His people, and He can be relied upon to keep those promises. Since He is faithful, we, too, should be faithful in our professions and our actions.

Is faith only a profession? No, it is also action because *"faith without works is dead"*

(James 2:20). Abraham was justified by his works when he offered Isaac on the altar. So, Abraham believed God (faith), and it was accredited to his account as righteousness. For that reason, he was called *"the Friend of God"* (James 2:23).

I want to be called the friend of God, how about you? We can only be called that as we remain a person of faith:

As the body without the spirit is dead, so faith without works is dead also.

James 2:26

In other words, faith is like our body, and works are like the spirit. There is no life in the body without the spirit, and no life in faith declarations without works.

If someone comes to you with a need, and you tell them to be warmed and filled and depart in peace, but don't meet the need with physical help, your faith is null and void. *"What doth it profit?"* (James 2:14 and 16). So, what can we conclude? Faith is a strong shield against the attacks of the enemy and is necessary to our survival and success as Christians.

THE HELMET OF SALVATION

Now let's look at another part of the armor of God which is included in the weapons of our warfare. It is called *"the helmet of salvation."*

The word *helmet* in the Greek language means "the protection of the soul which consists in (the hope of) salvation." In order to be protected from the onslaught of Satan and spiritual wickedness in high places, we must be saved.

Is it possible to take off the helmet of salvation? That is a theological argument that has gone on for ages, and I will not tackle it at this time. I have always personally felt that if you really know what you are doing when you accept Jesus as Savior, then you are saved. In other words, if you believe that Jesus is the Son of God and that He is God, and that He died for your sins, then you will be saved.

If you believe that all have sinned and come short of the glory of God and know that you also are a sinner, then you have to come to a conclusion. That conclusion is that you will also die spiritually and go to Hell. Why is that? Because if you believe that the penalty for sin is death, then you know you deserve death.

But when you believe that Jesus died to take your place, when you believe that He shed His precious blood to forgive you of your sin, then you truly believe in His saving grace for you. If you fully understand the ramifications of what God did for you and you accept His gift of eternal life, how in the world could you ever turn from Him? So, why are we admonished to *"put on"* the helmet of salvation?

Honestly, I do not know the answer to that question. All I can speculate is that it means to constantly bring to remembrance the wonderful gift of salvation that God has provided for us. And I imagine it is the same with putting on the other parts of the armor of God.

TAKING THE SWORD OF THE SPIRIT

There are two more pieces of the armor of God that had provided to enable us to stand against the wiles of the devil and help us defeat the enemy of fear. At first glance it appears that there is only one more part to the armor. I will talk about the sword of the Spirit first and then the last piece.

The sword of the Spirit is described in Ephesians 6:17: *"and take the helmet of salvation, and the sword of the Spirit, which is the Word of God."* The writer of Hebrews declared:

For the Word of God is quick, and powerful, and sharper than any two edged sword, piercing even to the dividing asunder of soul and spirit, and of the joints and marrow, and is a discerner of the thoughts and intents of the heart. Hebrews 4:12

This verse is a powerful one and has been preached and written about for centuries. Suffice it to say that the Word of God *is* the Sword of the Spirit.

The Word of God is also described as Jesus Christ Himself. For instance John wrote:

In the beginning was the Word, and the Word was with God, and the Word was God. John 1:1

Verses 2 through 27 perfectly describe that Jesus is the Word of God. Verse 14 says:

The Word was made flesh [Jesus] and dwelt among us, and we beheld His glory, the glory as of the only begotten of the Father, full of grace and truth.

So, the sword of the Spirit is the Word of God, and Jesus is the Word of God. No wonder then that we are admonished to take up the sword of the Spirit in our conflict with demonic forces. The enemy wants to paralyze us with fear, but we cannot give in to his tactics because that would allow him to win.

He most certainly will not win in the end. His end is prophesied in the book of Revelation. When we put on the armor of God, we actually cause the devil and his demons to run in fear. The enemy cowers at the appearance of a Christian cloaked in the armor of God. That's how powerful the Word of God is.

God's Word was first spoken by Him, and then it was written by men who were inspired by His Holy Spirit. Then all of these writings were collected and combined into what we now know as the Bible today.

God's word is powerful in another way. When He speaks, things happen. Genesis declared:

> *And God said, Let there be light: and there was light.*   Genesis 1:3

"God said." In other words, He spoke, and when He spoke, there was a manifestation of what He had spoken. His words caused something to be created out of nothing.

Verse 2 shows that there was darkness on the face of the deep, but God spoke in verse 3, and suddenly there was light. In verse 6, God *"said,"* and it was done. In verses 9, 11, 14, 22, and 24, God spoke, and what He spoke came to pass.

In verse 26, God spoke and said, *"Let us make man in our image, after our likeness,"* and it was so. This act of creation by God's words was true right on through the crowning glory of His creation, man:

> *So God created man in His own image.*
> Verse 27

Everything that exists was created through God's words:

> *Through faith we understand that the worlds were framed by the Word of God, so that things which are seen were not made of things which do appear.*
> Hebrews 11:3

In other words, God did not frame or form the world by starting with any physical material. He framed and formed the universes and all that it contains just by speaking His words.

God continued to speak throughout the remainder of the Bible, and things continued to happen. And today, God continues to speak to His people by His Holy Spirit, and when He speaks, things still happen. We just need to be close enough to Him to hear His still small voice. The Bible tells us that when we draw close to God, He draws close to us.

The Sword of the Spirit is a powerful weapon against our spiritual enemies, but it must be spiritually wielded by us, as Christians, through speaking God's Word against the enemy of our souls. One way we use that weapon is through prayer.

I will not elaborate here on the power of prayer because hundreds of books have been written on that important subject. However, I will briefly look at it as the final part of the armor of God mentioned in Ephesians 6:18. That passage ends this way:

Praying always with all prayer and supplication in the Spirit, and watching thereunto with all perseverance and supplication for all saints.

The apostle Paul wrote that he prayed in the Spirit and also with his understanding and that he sang in the Spirit and also with his understanding. No wonder, then, that he was such a powerful man. There is also a tremendous power to be experienced in praise and worship.

But our journey, as Christians, starts with a prayer of repentance and confession. It starts with our believing and confessing. It starts with us demonstrating faith in God. Jesus said:

Repent and believe the gospel.   Mark 1:15

Be not afraid, only believe.   Mark 5:36

All things are possible to him that be-lieves.   Mark 9:23

Do not doubt in your heart, but only be-lieve.   Mark 11:23

When you pray, believe that you will receive your answers, and you will.   Mark 11:24

These signs will follow them that believe.   Mark 16:17

God has given the power to become the sons of God to those who would believe in His name.   John 1:12

So, if we are encourage to *"put on"* the armor of God, that implies that we don't always have it on. If that is the case, then it is no wonder that we are sometimes unprotected against attack and ineffective in spiritual warfare against the enemy. The armor may seem heavy, but it is powerful and necessary.

Throughout the Bible we are encouraged to believe or have faith. Having faith in God and loving God and people are paramount to overcoming the spirit of fear.

Am I the only one who has ever had fear? No, I'm sure you have experienced it too. How would you rate your fear? On a scale of 1 to 10, what level would it be, with 1 being the least amount of fear and 10 being the most? Be honest.

For many of us, the level of fear changes as circumstances change. For some, fear is always at a high level. To these, I say, how would you like to live in a constant state of "fearlessness"? This may seem impossible, but I believe it is entirely possible through some of the things we have been discussing so far in this book. Why not give them a try?

Chapter 6

Choosing Fear or Faith?

And the Lord spake unto Moses, saying, Send thou men, that they may search the land of Canaan, which I give unto the children of Israel: of every tribe of their fathers shall ye send a man, every one a ruler among them.   Numbers 13:1-2

The Bible contains many stories of people who seemingly had no fears at all. There are also stories of those who had fears and yet overcame them. And, of course, there are stories of those who let their fears destroy them. Let's take a look at some of those stories.

God told Moses to send men to search out the land of Canaan (which He had already promised to the children of Israel). Moses responded by sending the heads of each individual tribe. He told them to spy out the people who dwelled in that land to see whether they were strong or weak, few or many. He also wanted them to check out the condition of the land, to see if it was bountiful or not and to bring back some of the fruit of the land.

The men went and searched out the land and returned after searching for forty days, bringing back a large cluster of grapes and some pomegranates and figs.

They presented their report to Moses and Aaron and the congregation of Israel and showed them the fruit of the land they had brought. They said that the land indeed flowed with milk and honey. However, they reported that the people of the land were strong and very great and that the cities were walled. The congregation of Israel was disturbed by this news, but one of the spies, a man named Caleb, a representative of the tribe of Judah, stilled them and said:

Let us go up at once, and possess it, for we are well able to overcome it.

Numbers 13:30

Caleb seemed to be exhibiting a total lack of fear.

The other leaders who had gone with him on this mission said something very different. In their opinion, they would *not* be able to take the land because the people there were stronger. The attitude of these men was one of fear, so they brought back an evil report. The land, they said, "*Ate up*" the inhabitants, and the people were giants of great stature. This had caused them, they said, to look at themselves as grasshoppers, and they felt the giants had looked at them the very same way. This evil report brought so much fear upon the congregation of Israel that the people lifted up their voices and wept.

The next day, the people murmured against Moses and Aaron and said they wished that God would have let them die in Egypt. They asked why God had brought them into this land to die by the sword and that their wives and children would become prey. Then they said to each other:

Let us make a captain, and let us return into Egypt.   Numbers 14:4

At this point, Moses and Aaron fell on their faces before the congregation of Israel, and Joshua and Caleb rent their clothes and pleaded with the people. The land they had searched out, they said, was a very good land, one that did indeed flow with milk and honey. And, they said, if God delighted in them, He would surely bring them into that promised land. They encouraged the people not to rebel against the Lord or to fear the people of the land. Rather, they assured, these people would be *"bread"* for them. They said:

> *Their defence is parted from them, and the* LORD *is. with us: fear them not.*
>
> Numbers 14:9

What was the reaction of the people of Israel to all of this? Instead of believing this powerful report of Joshua and Caleb, they wanted to stone them.

And that's when God showed up. Suddenly the glory of the Lord appeared in the tabernacle, and God asked Moses how long the people would provoke Him. He asked Moses how long it would be before these people would believe Him, considering all the signs He had shown them along their journey. Now, God said, He would smite them with pestilence and disinherit them and make the descendants of Moses into an ever greater nation.

But Moses reasoned with the Lord. If He did what He was saying, the Egyptians would hear of it and tell the inhabitants of the land (for they had heard that God was among the Israelites and that there was a cloud that was over them and went before them). In the daytime, God's presence was in that pillar of a cloud, and at night it was with them in a visible pillar of fire.

Moses now told God that if He killed the people the nations that had heard of His fame would say that He had killed them in the wilderness because He wasn't able to bring them into the land. Instead, Moses begged the Lord to forgive the people because of His great power, mercy, and long-suffering.

In response, God told Moses that He had pardoned the people, according to the word of His faithful servant. He assured Moses that, as truly as He lived, all the earth would be filled with the glory of the Lord.

You can read the rest of this great story in Numbers 22-38. Interestingly enough, the only two men of the older generation who did not die in the wilderness and who went on into the land were Joshua and Caleb. They were accompanied by the next generation of the people, those who did not die in the wilderness, those who were too young to doubt God.

The journey of the children of Israel in the wilderness, between Egypt and the Promised Land, should have taken them about eleven days. Instead, the people wandered in the desert for forty years. What a waste of an opportunity for a new life! They had been in bondage, as slaves in Egypt, for more than four hundred years, and God had set them free in a miraculous way, and now they had "blown" it.

So, out of that older generation, only Joshua and Caleb were left alive to bring the new generation into the Promised Land. Even Moses was only allowed to view the land, but could not go in to possess it. He had been used by God in mighty ways to deliver the people out of Egypt, but he could not enter the land because of fear, unbelief, and the consequent disobedience.

You may wonder how these people could have been so fearful, after seeing the great deliverances and miracles that God had done for them. Why did they stop believing Him? If they had persevered in their faith, they would have overcome their fears, and would have enjoyed the benefits of the Promised Land.

As Christians, why do *we* sometimes stop believing God? Is it because the answers to our prayers seem to take so long in coming? Do we perhaps give up too quickly?

On a personal level, let me share a short story about my Dad. He was a strong man of conviction. He was a wonderful husband and father of seven children. He was a Navy veteran who had fought in World War II. He founded and owned two successful companies, but then, because of employee theft, he lost his second company. He and his family had purchased land, which he knew would become valuable one day. Unfortunately, because of hard financial pressure and fear of financial collapse, he committed suicide in his sixties. Later, that land did become very valuable. Dad would have been a millionaire, but, instead, he never saw his vision fulfilled.

This is a sad story, but I share it here to make a point: How many times do we, as Christians, give up too soon? How many times do we allow fear to keep us from seeing our visions fulfilled? My purpose in writing this book is to help you to shake yourself and to see the power of Almighty God in a new way. I desire that you understand that God is for you, not against you. God wants you to be blessed in every area of your life. He has a great plan for you.

He said:

I know the thoughts that I think toward you, saith the Lord, thoughts of peace, and not of evil, to give you an expected end.
                                      Jeremiah 29:11

The word *expected* in the Hebrew means "a cord of hope or a hoped for outcome." Do you still hold out hope that all of God's promises will be fulfilled in you? If not, let hope rise in your right now. God is on your side.

CHAPTER 7

"BE NOT AFRAID OF THEIR FACES"

Be not afraid of their faces: for I am with thee to deliver thee, saith the Lord.

Jeremiah 1:8

God also encouraged the prophet Jeremiah not to be afraid. Let's look briefly at his story. It can be found in the book bearing his name.

In the opening words of the book, Jeremiah recorded that the Word of the Lord came to him, and God told him that before he had been formed in his mother's belly, He had known him, and before he had come out of the womb, He had sancti-fied him. God also said that He had ordained Jeremiah to be a prophet to the nations.

Jeremiah, in response, told God that he could not speak because he was just a child. Fear causes us to make many foolish excuses.

God told Jeremiah not to say that he was a child because he would go to all that God would send him, and he would speak whatever he was commanded. Then God commanded him: *"Be not afraid of their faces: for I am with thee to deliver thee saith the* LORD.*"* With God, nothing is impossible, and we can do all things through Christ which strengthens us. God is our strength and our power. We are weak in our own power, but strong in the power of the Lord.

God next touched Jeremiah's mouth:

Then the LORD *put forth His hand, and touched my mouth. And the* LORD *said unto me, Behold, I have put my words in thy mouth.*   Jeremiah 1:9

When we speak the words of the Lord to our situations, He causes things to change. **God empowers our words, when they are in alignment with His own Word.**

God went on to encourage Jeremiah and to tell him what he would do for Him. He told him that He had set him over the kingdoms and the nations to root out, pull down, destroy, and throw down. Also He said He would use Jeremiah to build and to plant. What Jeremiah would pull down and destroy was the idolatry of God's people. What he would build up and plant was God's Kingdom authority and the true and pure worship of Him.

The Lord then asked Jeremiah what he saw (in the Spirit). He said that he saw a rod of an almond tree. The almond tree signifies the first to arouse and wake from the sleep of winter. The emphasis is this discourse was on haste and ardor. The awakening in this scripture was in reference to God's people and the nation of Israel. God told him, in verse 12, that He would hasten His Word to perform it.

This was the good thing that Jeremiah saw, but he also saw something that was *not* good. God asked him the second time what he saw, and he said he saw a seething pot, and the face of it was toward the north. God told him that an evil would break forth out of the north upon all of the inhabitants of the land. He said that He would call all of the families of the kingdoms of the north, and that they would come and set up their thrones at the gates of Jerusalem, against all the walls and cities of Judah.

God went on to tell Jeremiah that He would utter His judgments against them for their wickedness, especially their worship of other gods. God told Jeremiah to *"gird up [his] loins"* and speak to them what He had commanded him. He told him, *"Be not dismayed at their faces,"* or He would confound him before them. This is a lesson for all Christians. We are not to be in fear to speak what God has told us to speak.

What has God told us to speak? His Gospel! If we do not proclaim His Gospel and His goodness and mercy, then God will confound us before the people.

In verse 18, God told Jeremiah that He had made him a defenced city, an iron pillar, and brazen walls against the whole land. God continues to tell us today that if we will speak His Word to the world He will make us a defenced city, iron pillars, and brazen walls against the naysayers and those who would reject the Gospel.

When we are attacked by those who will not accept God's unconditional love through His offering of His only Son, Jesus Christ, God will protect us. Be fearless to proclaim the good news (Gospel), for it is the power of God unto salvation.

God continued to use Jeremiah to speak to the people of Judah and Jerusalem, for them to repent and serve Him. Jeremiah was obedient, even though he had begun in fear. God can change your fear into faith, if you will take steps to obey Him.

Even simple obedience will help us to overcome the spirit of fear. And obedience to God's Word will keep us in alignment with His will for our lives. God knows what is best for us, and He has the perfect plan for us.

The Bible says:

Rebellion is as the sin of witchcraft,
                              1 Samuel 15:23

Rebellion to God's Word is the same as disobedience to His Word. Stubbornness is like iniquity and idolatry. 1 Samuel 15 describes how God stripped Saul's kingdom from him because of his disobedience, rebellion, and rejection of His Word. Even in the garden of Eden, Adam was disobedient to God, and sin came upon all because of that rebellion.

Disobedience is unacceptable to God, and a lack of repentance for it will bring God's wrath upon the children of disobedience (see Ephesians 5:6 and Colossians 3:6). We have confidence in God's protection for our lives, if we constantly remain obedient to His Word and His will. This confidence will cause us to trust Him more and to fear less.

Chapter 8

How Elijah Handled Fear

And Elijah came unto all the people, and said, How long halt ye between two opinions? if the Lord be God, follow him: but if Baal, then follow him. And the people answered him not a word.

1 Kings 18:21

Another prophet whom God called and used was Elijah. He was a mighty prophet, but he was not without fear. Let's look briefly at his story. You can read the account of his boldness and his fear starting with this verse.

Elijah came to the people and asked them how long they would be indecisive about who the true God was. If the Lord was God, then they should follow Him, but if Baal was God, then they should follow him.

According to Elijah, he was the only remaining prophet of the LORD, when Baal had four hundred and fifty prophets dedicated to him. Elijah now proposed a contest of sorts to determine which god was true.

He told the people to choose a bullock for them and two for him to burn upon the altar. They should then call on the name of their gods, and he would call on the name of the Lord, and the god who answered by fire would be accepted as God.

The prophets of Baal did as he said and called on the name of Baal from morning till noon, leaping on the altar. Of course, there was no answer by voice or fire. At noon, Elijah mocked them and said:

Cry aloud: for he is a god; either he is talking, or he is pursuing, or he is in a journey, or peradventure he sleepeth and must be awaked.   1 Kings 18:27

With this, the false prophets cried louder and cut themselves, and blood flowed from them. This went on until the evening, and yet there was no answer.

Then Elijah called the people to him to repair the broken altar. He took twelve stones, representing the twelve tribes of Israel, and made an altar in the name of the Lord. Then he made a trench around the altar. He put wood on the altar and cut up the bullock and laid it on the wood.

Now Elijah told the people to fill four barrels with water and pour them over the sacrifice and over the wood. Then he told them to do it a second and a third time. The water ran down the altar and filled the trench he had dug.

At the time of the evening sacrifice, Elijah called upon the Lord God of Abraham and said that he had done all these things at God's word. Then a wonderful thing happened:

Then the fire of the Lord fell, and consumed the burnt sacrifice, and the wood, and the stones, and the dust, and licked up the water that was in the trench.

1 Kings 18:38

The result was that the people fell on their faces and repeated, *"the Lord, He is the God."* Elijah then told the people to kill all the prophets of Baal, and they slew them at the brook Kishon.

King Ahab was over Israel at this time, but he was an evil ruler. By taking a heathen bride, Jezebel, the daughter of Ethbaal, King of the Zidonians, he had put himself in alignment with her, a Baal worshipper.

Elijah had just been fearless in killing the prophets of Baal, yet fear would soon come upon him. Ahab told Jezebel what Elijah had done, and she sent a messenger to Elijah:

So let the gods do to me, and more also, if I make not thy life as the life of one of them by to morrow about this time.

1 Kings 19:2

In other words, Jezebel was telling Elijah that she would kill him just like he had killed Baal's prophets. He immediately got up and ran for his life.

There are times when you may be fearless in one moment and full of fear the next. The things that cause one person to fear may not bother someone else. Elijah was terrified.

He went alone a days journey into the wilderness and sat down under a juniper tree and asked God to take his life. He fell asleep under that tree, because he was so exhausted from the trip. An angel touched him and woke him and told him to arise and eat. There was a cake baking on the coals and water at his head. So he ate and drank and went back to sleep.

The angel touched and woke him a second time and told him to arise and eat because the journey ahead was too great for him. Elijah did as he was told and went on the strength of that food for forty days and forty nights and arrived at Horeb, which was the mountain of God.

The prophet settled into a cave there, and the word of the Lord came to him and asked him what he was doing there. Elijah responded that the children of Israel had forsaken God's covenant, thrown down His altars, and slain His prophets and that he was the only one left, and now Jezebel was looking for him to kill him. God's man was having a pity party; in fear, he was ready to give up. How many times do we allow fear and hopelessness to bring us to the point of desperation and surrender?

God told Elijah to go and stand on the mountain before him. The Lord came by him and broke up the rocks of the mountain with a strong wind, but the Lord was not in the wind. Then an earthquake came, but the Lord was not in the earthquake. Then a fire came, but the Lord was not in the fire. After all these mighty and fearful things, God spoke to Elijah in a *"still small voice"* (1 Kings 19:12).

There are several messages a preacher could preach on these verses, but one that I think has not been spoken is this: the three things that happened all may have caused great fear in Elijah — the wind that broke up the rocks, the earthquake that could have killed him, and the fire that also could have devoured him. They were all natural events that inspired fear. But then God spoke to him in a still small voice. The voice of God is reassuring. The voice of God brings peace. The voice of God brings direction, and that was Elijah's deliverance.

What do we listen to these days? What gets our attention? God's still small voice to Elijah was what he needed. And God's still small voice is what we need to help us to overcome the temptation to give in to fear.

But how can we hear God's voice when there is so much noise around us? The noises of this world are louder than ever. The distractions in this world are multiplied by all types of media. It may be excessive television, movies, video games, cell phones, computers, or even people. There are all types of distractions that will keep us from hearing God's voice.

I believe in keeping up with the news and world events, but too much focus on them can cause fear. When every waking moment of every day is filled with "noise," it is virtually impossible to get the direction that we need for our lives. The direction that we receive from God is what we need to fulfill our destiny on this earth.

The direction we need from Him comes in the form of hearing His voice. We probably will not hear an audible voice, but if we ask Him to speak to us concerning His will and direction for our lives, He will answer. As noted earlier in the book, the Bible assures us that if we draw close to God, He will draw close to us (see James 4:8). We need to draw close enough to God to be able to hear His *still small voice.*

God is waiting to listen to us and to speak to us. That is one of His greatest desires. He wants us to love Him more than we love the world and its toys. When we are so focused on the things of this world, it causes us to actually worship them as idols, instead of worshiping the Creator of the Universe. I am in no way advocating giving up all entertainment, but if you have an abnormal amount of fear in your life, you may want to spend some quality time in the presence of God. He will give you His peace.

Personally, when I don't spend enough time in His presence, I feel like I am wasting my life away. I feel as if I were wasting the time that God has allotted to me.

How about you? You and I are the only ones who can decide how much time we will spend with God. It is up to us and requires a simple decision, a decision to either serve the world or serve God. It is a decision that will affect our level of fear or peace. What do you want: fear or peace? I choose the peace that passes all understanding.

Chapter 9

Peace That Passes Understanding

Be careful for nothing; but in everything by prayer and supplication with thanksgiving let your requests be made known unto God. And the peace of God, which passeth all understanding, shall keep your hearts and minds through Christ Jesus.

Philippians 4:6-7

In other words, *be careful for nothing* means don't worry about anything, but pray and talk to God, and He will give you a peace that you can't even explain.

He will *"keep"* you in His perfect peace, as Isaiah declared:

Thou wilt keep him in perfect peace, whose mind is stayed on thee: because he trusteth in Thee.   Isaiah 26:3

How wonderful it would be if we were *"kept"* in God's perfect peace every moment of every day! That would leave no room for fear. We need to keep our minds *"stayed"* on God.

Jesus is called The Prince of Peace:

For unto us a child is born, unto us a son is given: and the government shall be upon his shoulder: and his name shall be called Wonderful, Counselor, The mighty God, The everlasting Father, The Prince of Peace.
                                Isaiah 9:6

Some of the meanings of the word *peace* in this passage are "completeness in number;

safety, soundness in body; welfare, health, prosperity; peace, quiet, tranquility, contentment." Jesus is all of that to those who love Him.

Many times Jesus told the people around Him *"Go in peace,"* or *"Peace be unto you."* It was a common greeting of the day among the Jewish people. To His disciples, Jesus said:

Peace I leave with you, my peace I give unto you: not as the world giveth, give I unto you. Let not your heart be troubled, neither let it be afraid. John 14:27

These things I have spoken unto you, that in me ye might have peace. In the world ye shall have tribulation: but be of good cheer; I have overcome the world.
John 16:33

In this world we will have *"tribulation."* The word *tribulation* in this context means "a pressing together, pressure, oppression, affliction, persecution, and burden." There is no way around having problems in this world. It will happen to all of us. The difference in how we handle tribulation when it comes depends on whom we trust. Do we trust ourselves? Do we trust friends? Do we trust the wisdom of the world? It is God's wisdom that brings peace.

The wisdom of the world is no wisdom at all. In 1 Corinthians 1:20, Paul taught that God made foolish the wisdom of this world. Later, in that same book, he said:

For the wisdom of this world is foolishness with God. For it is written, He taketh the wise in their own craftiness.

1 Corinthians 3:19

Verse 20 shows that the thoughts of the wise are *"vain"* or empty. Let me encourage you to trust only God's wisdom when the pressures of this world come upon you. Call upon Him, and He will give you His wisdom.

The book of Proverbs has a lot to say about wisdom. Proverbs 1:7, for instance, says:

The fear of the LORD is the beginning of knowledge: but fools despise wisdom and instruction.

Psalm 111:10 says the same thing. In this psalm, the word *beginning* means "the first, the chief, the choice part." In Proverbs, it means "the beginning, the first time."

The fear of the Lord is different than the fear of the unknown. The word *fear*, as applies to the fear of the Lord, means "terror, respect, and reverence." Yes, we should have great respect for the Creator of the Universe, who holds our lives in His

hands. We want to stay in His hand because, as Hebrews 10:31 says:

It is a fearful thing to fall into the hands
of the living God.

So, to paraphrase these scriptures, the
terror, respect and reverence of the Lord
is the principal part of knowledge or wisdom. The main ingredient in receiving
God's wisdom for your life is to have a rev-
erential respect for Him.

God desires that you ask Him for wisdom. He wants you to have His wisdom
so that you can make the right decisions
in your life, decisions that lead to peace.
James wrote:

If any of you lack wisdom, let him ask
of God, that giveth to all men liberally
and upbraideth not; and it shall be given
him.   James 1:5

This word *upbraideth* means "to reproach or revile." *Revile* means "to assail with abusive language." God will not attack you if you ask for His wisdom. On the contrary, He desires that you ask. He is ready to give you His wisdom *"liberally"* — if you will just approach Him and ask for it.

When you receive the wisdom of God, then you are on your way to a life of peace and a reduction of fear. As we said early on, God did not give us a spirit of fear, but a spirit of power and love and a sound mind.

Which spirit did God give us? He gave us His Holy Spirit to live within us. His Holy Spirit is power in our lives. He is love within us. He creates a sound mind in us. All of these characteristics are available to us — if we will submit to the Lordship of Jesus Christ within. They are the opposite of the spirit of fear.

How many problems in our lives can become opportunities for success if we will just let the Holy Spirit have His way in us. Fear holds us back. Fear limits us. Fear causes uncertainty. Fear causes failure. How long will we give in to the enemy called fear when we have the power of God resident in us? It's time to stand up against fear and wake each day with a new boldness that will cause us to triumph in every situation.

CHAPTER 10

NEEDED: BOLDNESS

The wicked flee when no man pursueth:
but the righteous are bold as a lion.

Proverbs 28:1

Let's take a look briefly at this needed trait of boldness, as it relates to fear. According to Proverbs, *"the righteous are bold as a lion."* Why? Because Jesus is the Lion of the Tribe of Judah, and Christ within us is the power to be as bold as a lion.

Are we always as bold as the Word of God says we are to be? If not, then why not? What hinders us?

It is a common thing for us to lack boldness. We have to be encouraged by God to walk in the boldness He has provided for us. Even Moses was told to be strong and of good courage, to fear not nor be afraid of his enemies. God told him that He would go with him and not fail or forsake him.

Moses told Joshua to be strong and of good courage and to go in to inherit the Promised Land. Isn't it interesting that he told Joshua the same thing that God had told him. When God is with us, He will also go before us into battle against the wickedness that tries to destroy us.

God has a spiritual Promised Land for us and wants us to take what has been promised to us.

Paul wrote to the Roman believers:

What shall we say to these things? If God be for us, who can be against us?

Romans 8:31

Throughout the Bible God encouraged His people to be strong and of good courage.

David told his son Solomon to be strong and of good courage and to fear not and not be dismayed. Why? Because God would be with him until his work was finished.

God told Daniel to fear not, have peace, and to be strong.

In the New Testament, we find:

Finally, my brethren, be strong in the Lord, and in the power of His might.
Ephesians 6:10

We need this encouragement, because as humans, we are frail. We have many insecurities, some, more than others. These insecurities can be caused by many things, but they can also be controlled. If we will allow God to take full control of our lives, if we will live in the provision of His strength

109

for us, if we will submit to the mighty hand of God, if we will just believe that what He said about us is true, then we are in a position to walk in His power. We will be in a position to live our lives in peace and boldness, with power and fearlessness, because He is our strength!

God's Word declares:

I can do all things through Christ which strengtheneth me. Philippians 4:13

The way of the world is for men and women to be bold and fearless in their own ability. For some reason, people think that if they can just summon enough courage and self-will, they can then overcome any situation. There are countless books on self-help and being successful through focusing on how you think. Somehow humans think that they have all the power they need to control their own lives and destinies. The problem with this thinking is that people are relying on their own frail human minds, and there is not enough power in their own thinking to overcome in every situation.

Pride is the problem and I believe it started when Lucifer was cast out of Heaven. You probably know the story, as it is described in Isaiah 14. Lets look at verses 12-14:

How art thou fallen from heaven, O Lucifer, son of the morning! how art thou cut down to the ground, which didst weaken the nations! For thou hast said in thine heart, I will ascend into heaven, I will exalt my throne above the stars of God: I will sit also upon the mount of the congregation, in the sides of the north: I will ascend above the heights of the clouds; I will be like the most high. Yet thou shalt be brought down to hell, to the sides of the pit.   Isaiah 14:12-14

Lucifer, better known as Satan, was cast out of Heaven, along with one third of the angels. They were cast down to the earth, where they then became demons:

> *And the great dragon was cast out, that old serpent, called the Devil, and Satan, which deceiveth the whole world: he was cast out into the earth, and his angels were cast out with him.*　　Revelation 12:9

Verse 10 calls Satan *"the accuser of our brethren."* Satan's sin was pride. He felt that he could actually be like God, and he tempted Adam and Eve in the Garden of Eden with the same idea. He told Eve that if she ate of the tree in the midst of the garden (that God had told them not to eat of), she and Adam would have their eyes opened, and they would become as gods. Then they would know good and evil. Both Adam and Eve fell for the sin of pride because they wanted to be as wise as God.

Pride caused Lucifer to fall from Heaven. Pride caused Adam and Eve to fall from God's grace and be cast out of the garden. Pride is deadly. God's Word declares:

Pride goeth before destruction, and an haughty spirit before a fall.

Proverbs 16:18

Pride says that we can control our own lives in our own strength. This always leads to a fall and destruction, and then fear takes hold.

God's way is so much better. He desires that we trust in Him. He wants us to be bold, but in the power of *"His"* might – not our own. Why does God want this? God wants us to acknowledge Him. He wants us to reverence Him. He wants us to love Him. The Bible says:

We love him because he first loved us.

1 John 4:19

God is our Father. If you have kids, then you know the feeling of wanting your children's love to be returned. A good parent takes care of their children's physical, emotional, and spiritual needs and pours out love unto them. A good parent does not always give their children everything they want, because they know what the child really needs and what may be harmful to them.

God is the preeminent parent, the original parent of all mankind. He is love, and He loves. God loves us so much that He will take care of our needs, but not always all of our wants.

God knows what is good for us. He knows what will cause us to mature and grow into strong Christians. He won't force His will upon His children, but He will provide direction for us. He is our help in times of trouble. He is our High Tower, our Deliverer, our Strength, and our Source. God is awesome and deserving of all praise!

Trusting in God will bring peace to your life and freedom from fear. Why would anyone want to live life on their own? How many times have I failed on my own? Walking in our own strength is dependent upon our sometimes-frail strength. If we want to run our lives by ourselves without God's help, then we are open to the attack of the enemy of our souls.

Without God's help, we are doomed to defeat. Without God's help, we may achieve riches and fame, but at what cost? In this life, we are not guaranteed a certain amount of years. We are not guaranteed good health. There are no guarantees. And if we happen to live a long life and achieve success financially and with a good reputation without God's help, who really cares?

What is our legacy without God? What can we take into eternity after our physical bodies die? I, for one, desire a lasting and eternal legacy. I don't desire for the world to remember me. I desire for my Father in Heaven to look at me and say:

Well done, thou good and faithful servant.　　　　　Matthew 25:21 and 23

My desire is to make my Daddy in Heaven happy with my faithfulness as a servant.

Jesus told His disciples that if they wanted to be great in the Kingdom of Heaven, then they were to be servants of all. What does this have to do with fear? **One reason for fear is not having the assurance that when we fall, someone will pick us up.** That Someone is none other than the Almighty God of the Universe. If we are bold in the Lord and not ourselves, then we can do *"all things through Christ"* because He *"strengthens us."* When we live our lives in the boldness which God gives us, then we will have no fear:

The LORD is on my side; I will not fear: what can man do unto me.

Psalm 118:6

The Psalm continues:

It is better to trust in the LORD than to put confidence in man. Psalm 118:8

Human beings will always fail us, but God will never fail us. Following man is like the blind following the blind. Both will fall into a ditch. But when we follow Jesus, our steps are ordered by God Himself.

When we are in Christ and His Holy Spirit dwells in us, then we have unseen help from Heaven that we don't even know about. Thank God, for it makes all the difference in the world.

CHAPTER 11

HAVING OUR SPIRITUAL EYES OPENED

Fear not: for they that be with us are more than they that be. with them.

2 Kings 6:16

Let's take a brief look at a circumstance in the life of the prophet Elisha. The story can be found in 2 Kings chapter 6. It starts in verse 8, where the king of Syria was warring against Israel. He learned that Elisha, because he was a prophet, was telling the king of Israel what the Syrian king was saying in his bedchamber. He told his servants to find out where Elisha was, and they told him that Elisha was in Dothan. He then sent horses and chariots and a great host by night and surrounded that place.

Elisha's servant rose up early the next morning and saw that the Syrians had surrounded the city. He told Elisha about it and asked what they were going to do. It was then that Elisha gave this wonderful answer: *"Fear not: for they that be with us are more than they that be with them."* This was Elisha's faith.

Elisha then prayed that God would open his servant's eyes, and God answered that prayer. When the young servant's eyes were opened, he saw that the mountain was full of horses and chariots of fire all around Elisha. Because the servant's spiritual eyes were opened, he saw that they had a heavenly host all around them, ready to do battle against the Syrians.

When the Syrians eventually attacked, Elisha asked the Lord to smite them with blindness, and that is exactly what God did. Elisha was then able to lead his people on to Samaria.

As Christians, we often don't even realize that we have help in our times of need. If we could only realize this fact, then we could do what God has called us to do with NO FEAR! We need our spiritual eyes to be opened. If God is for us, who can successfully be against us (see Romans 8:31)? The answer has to be: no one.

The psalmist declared:

The chariots of God are twenty thousand, even thousands of angels: the LORD is among them, as in Sinai, in the holy place. Psalm 68:17

For He shall give His angels charge over thee, to keep Thee in all Thy ways". Psalm 91:11

I believe that each of us has a guardian angel that is with us at all times. In New

Testament times, the angel of the Lord released Peter from prison. He went and knocked on the door of the home of Mary, the mother of John Mark, where believers were gathered in prayer.

A maiden named Rhoda went to the door and heard Peter's voice, and she went and told those who were present who it was. They said she was mad, but when she insisted over and over that it was Peter, they said, *"It is his angel"* (Acts 12:15). These early believers understood that each individual Christian has a personal angel. As it turned out, it actually was Peter at the door, but what they said that day confirms that they believed in personal angels of protection.

Knowing the truth of God's Word will free you from the torment of fear. Knowing that God is *"for"* you and not *"against"* you will bring such a peace to your heart that you will have no more reason to fear. Trust Him today.

CHAPTER 12

THE WORK OF GOD'S SPIRIT IN US

For as many as are led by the Spirit of God, they are the sons of God.   Romans 8:14

The true sons of God are those who are *"led by the Spirit of God."* This is an important point. Let's look at the power of the Holy Spirit working in us, as it relates to fear and fearlessness.

Jesus cast devils out of people by the Spirit of God, and He did many signs and wonders by the power of the Spirit. The work of the Spirit began long before that, however, way back in Old Testament times.

Genesis, the book of beginnings, tells us that when the earth was still without form and void and darkness was upon the face of the deep, *"the Spirit of God moved upon the face of the waters"* (Genesis 1:2). Job, one of the earliest of Bible characters, said that the Spirit of God had made him and that the breath of the Almighty had given him life (see Job 33:4).

The Hebrew word for *spirit* throughout the Old Testament meant "breath, wind of heaven, breath of air." The Spirit of God is powerful. He is our very breath.

Paul said in Romans that God used him to perform many signs and wonders by the power of the Holy Spirit. He, too, gave credit to the Spirit for the works of Jesus and said that this same Spirit can work in us:

But if the Spirit of him that raised up Jesus from the dead dwell in you, he that raised up Christ from the dead shall also quicken your mortal bodies by his Spirit that dwelleth in you.   Romans 8:11

What we know today as the Godhead consists of the Father, the Son (Jesus), and the Holy Spirit. Right now, the Father is seated on His throne in Heaven, and Jesus is seated on His right side. The Holy Spirit is with them and in them, but He is also here with us and in us.

As is the Father and the Son, the Spirit of God is everywhere in the heavens and in the earth, and everywhere at one time. He is a spirit and cannot be contained in one place.

To put this truth into simpler terms: Romans 8:11 means that if the same all-powerful Holy Spirit of God that was able to raise up the dead body of Jesus Christ dwells in us who are Christians then the Holy Spirit will *"quicken"* our mortal bodies.

This word *quicken* means "to give life or restore to life; to spiritually give greater powers of life to our mortal bodies." *Mortality* means that we are subject to physical death, as the body of Christ was. The Holy Spirit of God was in Christ, even though His body was crucified and dead. That Spirit had the power to raise up the body of Jesus and restore Him to physical life. The same Spirit of God still has that power to give new life to our ever-dying bodies. His Spirit is in us.

The apostle Paul, in Colossians 1:26-27, taught that there was a mystery which was hidden from the ages and generations, but that God had now manifested it to the *"saints."* What did he mean by this? Every Christian is a saint. This fact is mentioned over and over in the New Testament. So this mystery is revealed to each of us.

The mystery revealed to the saints is called *"glorious"* in verse 27. What is this glorious mystery? It is that Christ is *"in"* you, the hope of glory!

The Spirit of Christ is not only *"with"* us, but is *"in"* us because we have chosen Christ and become Christians. That's what it means to be a saint.

This word *saint,* in this particular context, means "most holy thing." Now I don't look at myself and think that I am a "most holy thing," but the word *holy* simply means "set apart." When a non-believer changes and becomes a believer in Christ, he becomes holy, set apart, a saint. He or she is now set apart for God's work and for His service.

By *"the hope of glory,"* Paul meant that we have an expectation of entering into God's splendor, magnificence, excellence, preeminence, dignity, and grace. We have an expectation of entering into the very presence of God and His kingly majesty, His perfection, and His exalted state. What a glorious hope it is! And all of this is possible because of the life-giving power of the Holy Spirit who lives within us.

Now, if we really understand and believe that the all-powerful Spirit of the living God lives in us, then why would we ever fear? I think that the daily activities and concerns of our lives distract us from the fact that God is with us and He is for us. We need to continually remember that the power of God is within us. As noted earlier, if God is for us, who or what can successfully be against us (see Romans 8:31)? By the power of the Spirit that dwells in you, be free from fear today.

Chapter 13

Fear Begets Fear

For the thing which I greatly feared is come upon me, and that which I was afraid of is come unto me. Job 3:25

To my way of thinking, fear begets fear. In other words, the more we dwell on fear and give in to it, the more fear comes upon us. Fear begins in the mind and manifests in the body, and fear can actually paralyze the body. Fear can cause unusual physical symptoms.

I am living this book as I am writing it. About a week ago, I was sitting at a desk at my place of work, and I passed out and fell to the floor. I awoke in the hospital emergency room, with no memory of the blackout or the ambulance ride. A co-worker said that she saw me fall from the stool, hit the floor, and then began convulsing.

I had a myriad of tests done, but none of them showed any problems with my heart or brain. I was prescribed an anti-seizure medication and released. The next time I pulled up the file for this book in the computer, I read the last paragraph I had written. It said, *"Fear begins in the mind and manifests in the body. Fear can actually paralyze the body. Fear can cause unusual physical symptoms."* I don't think I was in fear at the time of the incident, but I was under a lot of pressure that day.

My hope is that, after reading this book, you will refuse to allow fear to have power over you. Personally, I am determined not to allow the fear of a possible future seizure to control my life. God is in control, not the spirit of fear.

Have you ever had this spirit come upon you? It's nothing to be embarrassed about. As noted early on, it is common to mankind, but Paul wrote:

God is not the author of confusion, but of peace. 1 Corinthians 14:33

The word *confusion* in this scripture means "instability, a state of disorder, disturbance." Fear brings instability, disorder, and disturbance. God is the author of peace, which is the opposite of fear.

If God is not the author of confusion, who is? I contend that it is Satan. He wants to steal from you, kill you, and destroy you. Satan hates God, and he hates you. He is jealous of God and of you.

Knowing this can cause fear, if you give in to it. But, as Christians, we know that no weapon formed against us shall prosper (see Isaiah 44:7). We know that greater is He that is in us (the Holy Spirit), than he that is in the world (the antichrist, who is Satan himself) (see 1 John 4:4). We know that we are the apple of God's eye and that He has us protected under the shadow of His wings (see Psalm 17:8). We are God's prized possessions.

Psalm 24:1 declares that the earth belongs to the Lord and the fulness thereof. It continues that the world is His and those that are in the world. Psalm 50:12 says the same thing. In other words, God owns the earth, or the world, but He also owns the fulness of the world. The fulness is what's in the world. That is us. Psalm 89:11 declares:

The heavens are thine, the earth also is thine: as for the world and the fulness thereof, thou hast founded them.

So, do the Scriptures repeat themselves when they say that God owns the whole world and also everything that's in it? No, I believe that the Word is saying that God not only owns everything, but He reserves us as His prized possessions, or His pocket change.

For example, when you get your paycheck, the entire amount is yours, but some funds must be allocated toward the mortgage. Some will go to utilities, food, and gas, etc. What's left over is your pocket change, which is yours to spend on whatever you want. God owns everything, but we are His pocket change. He can spend us on whatever He wants. He can use us for His special purposes. We are very special to Him.

As we have established over and over, God is love, and He loves His children who have put their trust in Him. Because of God's care for you, He watches over you to protect you from the attacks of the enemy. Does this mean you will not be attacked and sometimes hurt? No. In this world you will have tribulation, but Jesus said that He had overcome the world (see John 16:33).

Refuse to live in fear. Instead, live in the knowledge that God will keep your soul, no matter who or what may attack you.

If you *are* living in fear, today can be your day of deliverance. Today can be the start of a new life full of peace, joy, and contentment. It can start today and then be increased day by day. When you make the decision that you have had enough of living your life in fear, you can have a renewed life. It takes a decision – with the help of God's Holy Spirit – to come out of the bondage of fear.

God's Word is full of life. His Word is full of peace. His Word will keep you content and full of joy – if you will read it and hide it in your heart. Daily communication with God in the form of prayer will keep you in His will, and you will feel His presence and His concern for you.

God's truth will set you free from fear, but attaining ultimate freedom from fear is a lifelong commitment and a daily task. It requires effort on our part, invigorated by the life-giving power of the Holy Spirit.

Remember Paul's admonition:

Rejoice in the Lord always: and again I say, Rejoice. Let your moderation be known unto all men. The Lord is at hand. Be careful for nothing; but in everything by prayer and supplication with thanksgiving let your requests be made known unto God. And the peace of God, which passeth all understanding, shall keep your hearts and minds through Christ Jesus.

Philippians 4:4-7

When we fully put our trust in God, when we rejoice in Him, when we pray expecting answers and are thankful to Him, God will give us His peace, and His peace will defeat the enemy of FEAR.

FEAR NOT, my friend, for God is with you, and He is for you. He will go before you in every step of your life. He will never leave you or forsake you. Even when we feel alone and forsaken, we are never alone. Even when we feel that the heavens are like brass, He is always there. To paraphrase Psalm 46:1: *"God is our refuge and our strength, a very present help in trouble."*

Let not your heart be troubled. Let not your heart fail because of fear. Let not your heart be shaken. Let your heart be comforted by the power of the Holy Spirit.

In closing, this is my prayer for you, my friend:

Now the God of hope fill you with all joy and peace in believing, that ye may abound in hope, through the power of the Holy Ghost. Romans 15:13

Amen!

If you have been blessed by this book, you may contact me at:

skblyt@cox.net